Francis Frith's

NORTHUMBERLAND AND TYNE & WEAR

PHOTOGRAPHIC MEMORIES

Francis Frith's

NORTHUMBERLAND AND TYNE & WEAR

Clive Hardy

First published in hardback in the United Kingdom in 2000 by
The Francis Frith Collection®

Hardback edition
ISBN 1-85937-072-1

Reprinted in hardback 2001

Paperback edition 2001
ISBN 1-85937-281-3

Reprinted in paperback 2006

British Library Cataloguing in Publication Data

Northumberland and Tyne & Wear - Photographic Memories
Clive Hardy
ISBN 1-85937-281-3

The Francis Frith Collection
Frith's Barn, Teffont,
Salisbury, Wiltshire SP3 5QP
Tel: +44 (0) 1722 716 376
Email: info@francisfrith.co.uk
www.francisfrith.com

Printed and bound in Great Britain

Front Cover: **SUNDERLAND**, *The Bridges 1900* S263003t

The colour-tinting is for illustrative purposes only, and is not intended to be historically accurate

Every attempt has been made to contact copyright holders of illustrative material.
We will be happy to give full acknowledgement in future editions for any items not credited.
Any information should be directed to The Francis Frith Collection.

AS WITH ANY HISTORICAL DATABASE THE FRITH ARCHIVE IS CONSTANTLY BEING CORRECTED AND IMPROVED AND THE PUBLISHERS WOULD WELCOME INFORMATION ON OMISSIONS OR INACCURACIES

Contents

FRANCIS FRITH: *Victorian Pioneer*

FRANCIS FRITH, Victorian founder of the world-famous photographic archive, was a complex and multitudinous man. A devout Quaker and a highly successful Victorian businessman, he was both philosophic by nature and pioneering in outlook.

By 1855 Francis Frith had already established a wholesale grocery business in Liverpool, and sold it for the astonishing sum of £200,000, which is the equivalent today of over £15,000,000. Now a very rich man, he was able to indulge his passion for travel. As a child he had pored over travel books written by early explorers, and his fancy and imagination had been stirred by family holidays to the sublime mountain regions of Wales and Scotland. 'What a land of spirit-stirring and enriching scenes and places!' he had written. He was to return to these scenes of grandeur in later years to 'recapture the thousands of vivid and tender memories', but with a different purpose. Now in his thirties, and captivated by the new science of photography, Frith set out on a series of pioneering journeys to the Nile regions that occupied him from 1856 until 1860.

INTRIGUE AND ADVENTURE

He took with him on his travels a specially-designed wicker carriage that acted as both dark-room and sleeping chamber. These far-flung journeys were packed with intrigue and adventure. In his life story, written when he was sixty-three, Frith tells of being held captive by bandits, and of fighting 'an awful midnight battle to the very point of surrender with a deadly pack of hungry, wild dogs'. Sporting flowing Arab costume, Frith arrived at Akaba by camel sixty years before Lawrence, where he encountered 'desert princes and rival sheikhs, blazing with jewel-hilted swords'.

During these extraordinary adventures he was assiduously exploring the desert regions bordering the Nile and patiently recording the antiquities and peoples with his camera. He was the first photographer to venture beyond the sixth cataract. Africa was still the mysterious 'Dark Continent', and Stanley and Livingstone's historic meeting was a decade into the future. The conditions for picture taking confound belief. He laboured for hours in his wicker darkroom in the sweltering heat of the desert, while the volatile chemicals fizzed dangerously in their trays. Often he was forced to work in remote tombs and caves where conditions were cooler. Back in London he exhibited his photographs and was 'rapturously cheered' by members of the Royal Society. His reputation as a photographer was made overnight. An eminent modern historian has likened their impact on the population of the time to that on our own generation of the first photographs taken on the surface of the moon.

Venture of a Life-Time

Characteristically, Frith quickly spotted the opportunity to create a new business as a specialist publisher of photographs. He lived in an era of immense and sometimes violent change. For the poor in the early part of Victoria's reign work was a drudge and the hours long, and people had precious little free time to enjoy themselves.

Most had no transport other than a cart or gig at their disposal, and had not travelled far beyond the boundaries of their own town or village. However, by the 1870s, the railways had threaded their way across the country, and Bank Holidays and half-day Saturdays had been made obligatory by Act of Parliament. All of a sudden the ordinary working man and his family were able to enjoy days out and see a little more of the world.

With characteristic business acumen, Francis Frith foresaw that these new tourists would enjoy having souvenirs to commemorate their days out. In 1860 he married Mary Ann Rosling and set out with the intention of photographing every city, town and village in Britain. For the next thirty years he travelled the country by train and by pony and trap, producing fine photographs of seaside resorts and beauty spots that were keenly bought by millions of Victorians. These prints were painstakingly pasted into family albums and pored over during the dark nights of winter, rekindling precious memories of summer excursions.

The Rise of Frith & Co

Frith's studio was soon supplying retail shops all over the country. To meet the demand he gathered about him a small team of photographers, and published the work of independent artist-photographers of the calibre of Roger Fenton and Francis Bedford. In order to gain some understanding of the scale of Frith's business one only has to look at the catalogue issued by Frith & Co in 1886: it runs to some 670

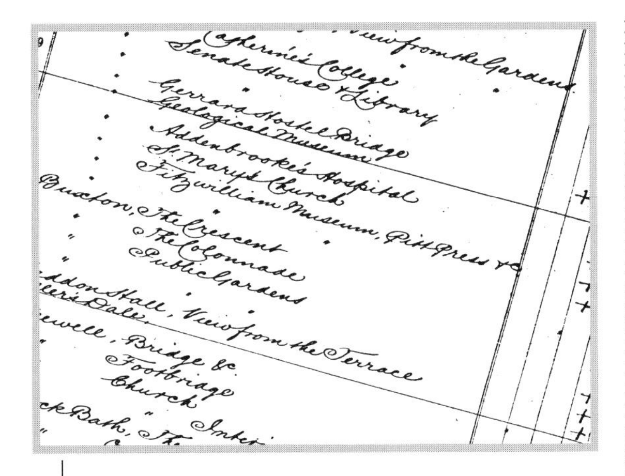

Senate House & Library
Geological Museum
Addenbrooke's Hospital
St Mary's Church
Fitzwilliam Museum, Pitt Press &c
The Crescent
The Colonnade
Public Gardens
View from the Terrace
Bridge &c
Footbridge
Church

pages, listing not only many thousands of views of the British Isles but also many photographs of most European countries, and China, Japan, the USA and Canada – note the sample page shown above from the hand-written *Frith & Co* ledgers detailing pictures taken. By 1890 Frith had created the greatest specialist photographic publishing company in the world, with over 2,000 outlets – more than the combined number that Boots and WH Smith have today! The picture on the right shows the *Frith & Co* display board at Ingleton in the Yorkshire Dales (left of window). Beautifully constructed with a mahogany frame and gilt inserts, it could display up to a dozen local scenes.

Postcard Bonanza

The ever-popular holiday postcard we know today took many years to develop. In 1870 the Post Office issued the first plain cards, with a pre-printed stamp on one face. In 1894 they allowed other publishers' cards to be sent through the mail with an attached adhesive halfpenny stamp. Demand grew rapidly, and in 1895 a new size of postcard was permitted called the court card, but there was little room for illustration. In 1899, a year after Frith's death, a new card measuring 5.5 x 3.5 inches became the standard format, but it was not until 1902 that the divided back came into being, with address and message on one face and a full-size illustration on the other. *Frith & Co* were in the vanguard of postcard development, and Frith's sons Eustace and Cyril continued their father's monumental task, expanding the number of views offered to the public and recording more and more places in Britain, as the coasts and countryside were opened up to mass travel.

Francis Frith died in 1898 at his villa in Cannes, his great project still growing. The archive he created continued in business for another seventy years. By 1970 it contained over a third of a million pictures of 7,000 cities, towns and villages. The massive photographic record Frith has left to us stands as a living monument to a special and very remarkable man.

Frith's Archive: *A Unique Legacy*

Francis Frith's legacy to us today is of immense significance and value, for the magnificent archive of evocative photographs he created provides a unique record of change in 7,000 cities, towns and villages throughout Britain over a century and more. Frith and his fellow studio photographers revisited locations many times down the years to update their views, compiling for us an enthralling and colourful pageant of British life and character.

We tend to think of Frith's sepia views of Britain as nostalgic, for most of us use them to conjure up memories of places in our own lives with which we have family associations. It often makes us forget that to Francis Frith they were records of daily life as it was actually being lived in the cities, towns and villages of his day. The Victorian age was one of great and often bewildering change for ordinary people, and though the pictures evoke an impression of slower times, life was as busy and hectic as it is today.

We are fortunate that Frith was a photographer of the people, dedicated to recording the minutiae of everyday life. For it is this sheer wealth of visual data, the painstaking chronicle of changes in dress, transport, street layouts, buildings, housing, engineering and landscape that captivates us so much today. His remarkable images offer us a powerful link with the past and with the lives of our ancestors.

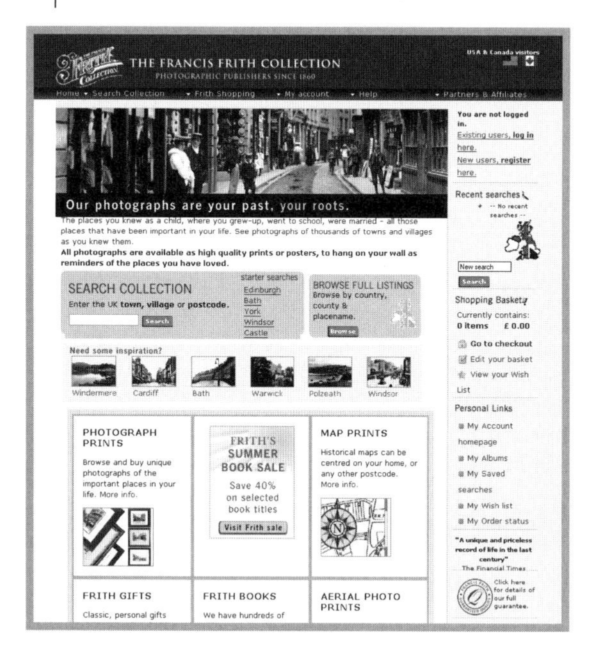

See Frith at www.francisfrith.com

Today's Technology

Computers have now made it possible for Frith's many thousands of images to be accessed almost instantly. In the Frith archive today, each photograph is carefully 'digitised' then stored on a CD Rom. Frith archivists can locate a single photograph amongst thousands within seconds. Views can be catalogued and sorted under a variety of categories of place and content to the immediate benefit of researchers. Inexpensive reference prints can be created for them at the touch of a mouse button, and a wide range of books and other printed materials assembled and published for a wider, more general readership - in the next twelve months over a hundred Frith local history titles will be published!

The day-to-day workings of the archive are very different from how they were in Francis Frith's time: imagine the herculean task of sorting through eleven tons of glass negatives as Frith had to do to locate a particular sequence of pictures! Yet the archive still prides itself on maintaining the same high standards of excellence laid down by Francis Frith, including the painstaking cataloguing and indexing of every view.

It is curious to reflect on how the internet now allows researchers in America and elsewhere greater instant access to the archive than Frith himself ever enjoyed. Many thousands of individual views can be called up on screen within seconds on one of the Frith internet sites, enabling people living continents away to revisit the streets of their ancestral home town, or view places in Britain where they have enjoyed holidays. Many overseas researchers welcome the chance to view special theme selections, such as transport, sports, costume and ancient monuments.

We are certain that Francis Frith would have heartily approved of these modern developments, for he himself was always working at the very limits of Victorian photographic technology.

The Value of the Archive Today

Because of the benefits brought by the computer, Frith's images are increasingly studied by social historians, by researchers into genealogy and ancestory, by architects, town planners, and by teachers and schoolchildren involved in local history projects. In addition, the archive offers every one of us a unique opportunity to examine the places where we and our families have lived and worked down the years. Immensely successful in Frith's own era, the archive is now, a century and more on, entering a new phase of popularity.

The Past in Tune with the Future

Historians consider the Francis Frith Collection to be of prime national importance. It is the only archive of its kind remaining in private ownership and has been valued at a million pounds. However, this figure is now rapidly increasing as digital technology enables more and more people around the world to enjoy its benefits.

Francis Frith's archive is now housed in an historic timber barn in the beautiful village of Teffont in Wiltshire. Its founder would not recognize the archive office as it is today. In place of the many thousands of dusty boxes containing glass plate negatives and an all-pervading odour of photographic chemicals, there are now ranks of computer screens. He would be amazed to watch his images travelling round the world at unimaginable speeds through network and internet lines.

The archive's future is both bright and exciting. Francis Frith, with his unshakeable belief in making photographs available to the greatest number of people, would undoubtedly approve of what is being done today with his lifetime's work. His photographs, depicting our shared past, are now bringing pleasure and enlightenment to millions around the world a century and more after his death.

NORTHUMBERLAND AND TYNE & WEAR – *An Introduction*

WELCOME TO THE Frith Collection and our selection of pictures relating to Northumberland, Tyne & Wear. It goes without saying that this is a part of England steeped in history: along with Yorkshire, it once formed the powerful Anglo-Saxon kingdom of Northumbria. Ruled from York, Northumbria by the early 7th century extended from the Forth to the Humber and the north bank of the Mersey. Indeed, it is thought that Edinburgh was founded in the 7th century by King Edwin. It is known that Edwin fortified a part of the hill where the present-day Edinburgh Castle stands, and he may also have encouraged civilian settlement nearby. Under another 7th-century king, Aethelfrith, Northumbria was powerful enough to launch an all-out assault on the city of Chester in 616 and hold onto it for about thirty years.

Northumbria, however, was always at a disadvantage. To the south were other Anglo-Saxon kingdoms; to the north and west were the kingdoms of the Scots, Strathclyde Welsh and Cumbrians. There was no love lost between Northumbria and the southern English, who regarded their northern kinsmen as bloody-minded, rebellious, cattle-raiding, beer-swilling good-for-nothings, who spoke dialects so coarse as to be incomprehensible to the majority of outsiders. It is true that life in the north for many was extremely hard and often brutal, but Northumbria was a kingdom rich in traditions. York was second in size and wealth only to London, and Holy Island was the birthplace of Christianity in England.

Northumbria would remain an independent kingdom until the early decades of the 10th century. By 920, Edward the Elder of Wessex had effectively destroyed the military strength of the Danelaw and had been grudgingly acknowledged as overlord by Danes and Northumbrians alike. However, the idea of a unified England did not go down well with everyone: the Mercians of Cheshire, aided by the Welsh, rose in armed revolt in 922. Edward was still attempting to crush the rebellion when he died at Farndon in 924. He was succeeded by Athelstan, a daring, resourceful, and when necessary totally ruthless soldier-politician. In 927 Sihtric, Norse-Irish king of York, died. Athelstan seized the moment and invaded. York was taken, and for the first time ever a South Angle king ruled between the Humber and the Tees. The land north of the Tees was effectively ruled from Bamburgh by Earl Ealdred Ealdulfing; but Ealdulfing, along with Constantine, king of the Scots, Donald, king of the Strathclyde Welsh, and Owain, king of the Cumbrians all submitted to Athelstan. By April 928 both the North Welsh and the Britons of Cornwall had also surrendered. But there was plenty of unrest. In 937 Athelstan destroyed a combined Scots, Danish and Welsh army at a place called Brunanburh, which was followed by a short period of peace until his death 939. The old antagonisms re-emerged. Northumbria again asserted itself, and continued to do so until the death in battle in 954 of its last king Eric Bloodaxe.

For centuries the exact border between Scotland and England was difficult to define; even William the Conqueror's Domesday Commissioners did not go north of the Tees. During the reign of his son William Rufus, England's northern frontier might well have followed the line of Hadrian's Wall, its focal points being the fortresses of Carlisle in the west, and the New Castle on the north bank of the Tyne over to the east. The castle on the Tyne had been built by Robert Curthose, the brave but short-tempered and headstrong eldest son of the Conqueror, on his return from campaigning against Malcolm III of Scotland. It was a motte and bailey: a wooden tower on a mound was protected by a ditch on its west side and by precipitous banks on the other three, and it was from this fortification that Newcastle would derive its name.

During the reign of David I, the Border was on the Tees; the Scots had gained territory not through force of arms but by skilful diplomacy. Later, when Henry II insisted that Northumbria be returned to England, William the Lion launched an invasion; but he was unfortunately captured at Alnwick and taken to the fortress of Falaise in Normandy. William acknowledged Henry as his feudal lord, and a number of castles in southern Scotland were ceded to the English. By the end of the reign of Edward I, the border was on a line from Carlisle to Berwick, both sides divided into three marches, each governed

by a Warden. The idea was that the Wardens would maintain law and order and meet with their respective opposite numbers in order to resolve any problems affecting their areas of control. That was the idea, but the practice was often different. There was also a vast expanse of land inland from the Solway Firth that was claimed by both crowns, though neither had any effective control over it. So turbulent was the North that of the 900 stone castles known to have been built in England over 200 were sited in Northumberland.

Years and years of devastation resulting from the coming and going of Scottish and English armies had reduced the Borders to a lawless no man's land where raiding, cattle reiving and sheep lifting had become a way of life. The Borderers themselves were not organised by nationality; Scots raided Scots, English raided English, Scots joined forces with English Borderers to raid other Scots and so on. Also, there were a number of Border clans, such as the Maxwells, Johnstones, Douglases, Armstrongs and Crichtons, who not only wreaked havoc throughout the area but fought pitched battles against one another, or were drawn into blood feuds that could last for decades.

Many of the Wardens were no better, often mounting raids of their own. There were, however, truce days when both sides met at an appointed place and matters were supposed to be resolved without men reaching for their swords. One truce that degenerated into a pitched battle was at Reidswire in the summer of 1575. The English were represented by their middle march warden Sir John Forster, a cunning old rascal in his seventies; his opposite number on the Scottish side was Sir John Carmichael, keeper of Liddesdale. After several hours of fairly amicable conversation an argument developed, which led to insults being exchanged and then blows. With one man dead, the wardens managed to calm down their followers, but suddenly the Scots jumped the English, capturing old Sir John and killing his deputy Sir George Heron. The English Borderers opened fire with longbows cutting down a number of Scots; the Scots in turn were reinforced by the arrival of men from Jedburgh, many no doubt carrying murderous Jedburgh axes with 4 ft long blades. It was the Scots' turn to attack, and they routed the English.

The castles in the Borders are for the most part tower houses on the Scottish side and Northumbrian peles on the English. Powerful clans were able to build fortresses such as Caerlaverock, seven miles south-south-east of Dumfries, built by the Maxwells, while the Douglases were responsible for fortifying Hermitage Castle. Throughout the Borders farmers, who were not only on the receiving ends of raids even from their own countrymen, but were often raiders and reivers themselves, took to building bastels for their protection. These were stone-built farmhouses, usually two-storey, their name derived from the French word bastille, a small fortress. The basement was for cattle and stores, the upper floor for domestic quarters. Those who could afford it built their bastels with barrel-vaulted basements and stone or slate roofs, as raiders often resorted to the use of fire. Even if raiders gained access to the basement, the vaulting was tough enough to prevent them breaking into the domestic quarters and butchering its occupants. The windows of the basement were the smallest possible, allowing in the bare minimum of light and ventilation. Windows in the domestic quarters were protected with iron bars. In Northumberland there are also examples of fortified vicarages, and the roof of St Cuthbert's Church in Bellingham was rebuilt with stone, either as a fire prevention measure, or to make the building a little more secure for villagers during a raid. When James VI of Scotland became James I of England the pacification of the Borders began. Troops poured into the area and justice was often swift and brutal. The reivers were effectively put out of business by 1610.

It was not until 1890 that a Frith cameraman was sent to the north-east, and even then the visit appears to have been confined to trips round Newcastle and Sunderland. Nothing of Northumberland's historic past was photographed; the assignment seems to have been simply one of taking pictures of suitable subjects for postcards that would sell in large numbers - hence the views of Grainger Street, the Quayside, Grey Street and so on. Bamburgh Castle, Belsay Old Castle, Craster, Alnwick, and Blanchland were not photographed until around 1950, and Corbridge, Cullercoats, Felton, Seahouses and Seaburn all had to wait until around 1955.

Frith cameramen made a number of visits to the north-east between 1950 and 1965. It was still a major industrial area. There were dozens of coal mines in operation; shipyards still lined the banks of the Tyne and the Wear; and railway locomotives were being built at Gateshead, turbines at Heaton, and armoured vehicles at Elswick. Townships often depended upon one large employer to provide most of the local jobs which in turn fuelled the local economy.

At the beginning of the 20th century British shipyards were at the forefront of world shipbuilding and the ship repair industry. The Russo-Japanese war of 1904-05 saw the R & W Hawthorn Leslie-built warships of Tsarist Russia take on and lose to the Vickers, Son & Maxim-built battleships of Imperial Japan. In those days British yards could build a battleship twice as fast as any American yard, and five times faster than those of the embryonic Japanese shipbuilding industry. Thousands found work in the yards on the Tyne and Wear. In 1903 Swan, Hunter & Wigham Richardson was formed at Wallsend from the amalgamation of the yards of Charles Swan & Hunter, and Wigham Richardson & Co. The new shipbuilding giant also purchased the intervening yard of the Tyne Ship & Pontoon Co to give a continuous river frontage, and took a majority holding in the marine engine building firm Wallsend Slipway and Engineering.

Across the Tyne at Jarrow was an older giant, the famous yard of Palmer Bros, founded in 1851 by brothers Charles and George Palmer to build colliers to ship coal to London. In 1852 the yard turned out the world's first sea-going screw collier for mine owner John Bowes of Barnard Castle. Carrying 650 tonnes of coal per trip, she could do the work of eight sailing colliers. The firm expanded rapidly, acquiring 14 of its own coalmines as well as its own ironstone company, and also interests in firms that supplied ships' fittings. From 1860 until 1912 Palmers also operated a yard at Howdon, where a considerable number of ships were built. After George Palmer retired, Charles continued to develop the business, opening an engine works, blast furnaces and iron and steel works. The company, which had gone public in 1865, was always innovative. In 1906 electric overhead cranes were installed, and in 1911 the seven-berth Hebburn yard of Robert Stephenson & Sons was leased and eventually purchased. Other acquisitions included a small yard at Amble and the building of a dry dock at Swansea for Palmers (Swansea) Dry Dock Co.

In 1930 output from British yards totalled 1.4 million tonnes. By 1933, as the Depression hit, it had slumped to 133,000 tonnes. Palmers completed their last merchant ship order in April 1931 and their last warship in 1933. With no prospect of orders, the company went into liquidation. It was a complete closure: shipyard, blast furnaces, rolling mills and engine works. Palmers passed into the

hands of the National Shipbuilders' Security, a controversial organisation set up by the industry to administer self-inflicted surgery to reduce shipbuilding capacity. Yards were bought and then demolished. The owners were compensated, while their former employees got nothing.

The effect upon Jarrow was disastrous: Palmers was Jarrow. The town was left with nothing, it had the highest rate of unemployment in the entire country, and the government, as usual, offered no help. Men wandered around looking for work that did not exist, while wives and mothers had little time to stand on street corners feeling sorry for themselves - they were forced to scrimp and scrape, beg or borrow in the attempt to feed and clothe their children.

There were to be many hunger marches during the 1930s; yet despite being one of the smallest, limited to just 200 men, the Jarrow Crusade has come down to us as being synonymous with the plight of the North-East during the Depression. Organised by the town council and local MP Ellen Wilkinson, the Crusade was an attempt to get the government to take notice of the dire straits Jarrow had been left in with the closure of Palmers. It was left to one man to come to the town's aid. In 1933 Sir John Jarvis, High Sheriff of Surrey, was so moved that he bought a ship due for scrapping and sent it to Palmers. The following year Sir John paid £100,000 for the White Star liner Olympic and then offered her to a Yorkshire scrap metal company for the same amount, providing they agreed to the demolition being done at Palmers. Olympic arrived on the Tyne in October 1935 and provided men with work for eighteen months. Sir John repeated his generous act in 1938 when he bought the Cunard liner Berengaria and sent her to Jarrow for breaking up.

Over on the Wear were a number of yards including William Doxford & Sons, Joseph Thompson & Sons, Short Brothers, and Sir John Priestman & Co. Sir John Priestman, born at Bishop Auckland in 1855, began his career at the age of fourteen when he was taken on as an apprentice at the shipyard of John Blumer & Co. After a period as Chief Draughtsman at Pickersgills, John opened his own yard at Southwick in 1882 and completed five ships by the middle of 1883. In 1897 the yard completed the first of their 'Towerdeck' self-trimming tramps, similar in style to Doxford's 'Turret' ships; these were designed to save shipowners money on Suez Canal dues, which were charged by deck area. John Priestman became one of Sunderland's great benefactors. He paid for the construction of St Andrew's Church, Roker, and the rebuilding of St Michael's, Bishopwearmouth. During his life his donations to charitable causes on Wearside amounted to over £500,000, and on his death further money was left in Trust for charitable work.

It was not all collieries and shipyards, for much of the landscape was developed for agriculture during the late-18th to mid-19th centuries and remains so to this day. Fishing, too, was once important to the economies of places like Craster, Alnmouth, Cullercoats, and North Shields. In the years immediately prior to the Great War Northumberland fishing ports were landing in excess of 450,000 cwt of white fish a year: cod, haddock, whiting, ling, halibut, sole, catfish, dab, plaice, conger eel, coalfish, and skate. On top of this were catches of mackerel, crabs, lobsters, and periwinkles. The top ports for white fish were North Shields, Blyth and Newbiggin; for crabs it was Beadnell, Craster, Cullercoats, Holy Island and North Sunderland. In the early 1920s there were nearly sixty trawlers operating out of North Shields; Richard Irwin & Sons were at their peak in 1939 with a fleet of 39 vessels.

Few things, however, remain the same, and industrialisation changed the face of many a town and village; others, like Ashington, grew out of nothing. All there was at Ashington until the coal company arrived on the scene was a single farm. Other places that owe their growth to mining include Killingworth, Shilbottle, Seghill, Backworth, Annitsford, and Cowpen. In complete contrast, the village of Belsay was demolished by Sir Charles Monck of Belsay Castle and relocated on the main road. The new village consisted on one long terrace featuring an arcaded ground floor, reflecting Sir Charles's taste for things Italianate. After all, he was wealthy enough to take two years for his honeymoon, wandering around Germany and the Mediterranean.

Wallsend is yet another ancient site. Situated at the eastern end of Hadrian's Wall, it was here that the Roman fort of Sedgedunum once stood. In the 17th century there was some glass manufacturing at Wallsend, but the town would owe its development to coal and shipbuilding. Wallsend Colliery was started by a Quaker family, but they ran into financial difficulties; they finished up having to borrow money from a Sunderland timber merchant by the name of William Russell. As soon as the pit shaft was sunk, Russell foreclosed the mortgage and took over the pit. Eventually Russell would own seven pits around Wallsend, and would make enough money to buy Brancepath Castle. The last pit in the town, Rising Sun Colliery, was proclaimed by the NCB to be one of its long-life pits, yet it was closed in April 1969 and demolished in 1974.

Between 1870 and the start of the Great War, Wallsend's population rocketed from 10,400 to over 41,000. Land was needed for housing, and nothing was sacred. Even the ruins of Sedgedunum had to go, though not without a fight. William Boyd, the borough's first mayor, attempted to organise a fund to buy the field in which the remains of the Roman fort stood. The owners wanted £680, which Boyd did not have - but the builders did. The builders moved in and destroyed what was left of the old fort; the rubble was used for the roads.

Wallsend's local church was the Holy Cross at Willington Gut. In the late 18th century it was in a sorry state, and a local landowner said he would pay to have the place repaired. The roof was stripped off, and that was the last the natives saw of their supposed benefactor. With the church now utterly useless, a schoolroom was pressed into service. All went well for about ten years. Then in 1806 the Dean and Chapter of Durham caused chaos by announcing that the schoolroom had not been consecrated and that thus all weddings that had taken place there were invalid. That was not all, for the Church declared that all the couples were deemed to be living in sin, and that all the children born to them were bastards. The result was the building of St Peter's, in somewhat indecent haste, on the hill above the ropeworks. As for the Holy Cross, it faired little better than Sedgedunum. By 1968 what little there was left of the 800-year-old church was in danger of becoming nothing more than a heap of rubble due to vandalism. As the ruin measured just 52ft x 21ft, the Ministry of Public Buildings & Works refused to allow it to be scheduled as an ancient monument.

This book is in no way an academic history. The introduction is simply to set the scene, while the pictures and their associated captions will, we hope, give an enjoyable tour of this fascinating area.

BERWICK-UPON-TWEED
The Royal Tweed Bridge c1960 B305037

The 1405ft long concrete four-span Royal Tweed Bridge, designed by L G Mouchel & Partners, was built in 1925-28 to take traffic off the old stone bridge that still stands nearby. The old bridge dates from the 17th century. It has fifteen segmented arches of varying height and width; it is 1168 ft long and built of red sandstone. There is a third bridge at Berwick. It is Robert Stephenson's magnificent 28-arch Royal Border of 1850, which carries the railway 120ft above the river. It took three years to build, but when completed it allowed through running of trains between Edinburgh and Newcastle-upon-Tyne.

Berwick-upon-Tweed
The Lighthouse 1965
64 miles north of Newcastle, Berwick was a principal port for the importing of grain and timber. The pier dates from 1810-21, and the lighthouse was added in 1826.

Holy Island c1955
A Tudor fort sitting on top of Beblowe Crag, Lindisfarne was raised for defence against the Scots. Construction began in 1542 and was completed by 1550, using stone salvaged from the Benedictine priory. The only action the castle ever saw was when it was 'captured' from its garrison of just seven men by two Jacobites, who then flew their flag for a few hours before they were eventually thrown out. The castle was demilitarised in 1819; in 1902 it was converted into a private residence for Edward Hudson by Sir Edwin Lutyens.

Berwick-upon-Tweed, The Lighthouse 1965 B305038

Holy Island c1955 H348112

BAMBURGH, ST CUTHBERT'S CHAPEL, FARNE ISLANDS c1935 B547021
According to Bede, St Aidan retired to Inner Farne for solitude, and St Cuthbert died here in AD687. A Benedictine cell from Durham was established here in 1246, and a chapel dedicated to St Cuthbert was built in 1370. After buying the islands in the 19th century, Archdeacon Thorp set about a heavy restoration of the chapel, which included using second-hand panelling and pews from Durham Cathedral.

BAMBURGH, THE VILLAGE AND THE CASTLE c1955 B547022
The Norman keep with its four corner turrets, similar to that at Rochester, was built between 1164 and 1170. Though it looks impressive, the keep is in fact only 35ft high, about a third of the height of those at fortresses like Scarborough and Richmond, and is nearly square at 69ft x 61ft.

BAMBURGH CASTLE c1960 B547029
A fortified site since the 8th century, the Norman castle at Bamburgh was besieged in 1095 by William II. Unable to take the fortress from Robert de Mowbray, third Earl of Northumberland, William headed south, leaving the prosecution of the siege to others. Mowbray attempted to escape, but was captured. His wife only surrendered Bamburgh after her husband had been paraded before the walls under threat of having his eyes torn out.

Bamburgh Castle c1960 B547030

In July 1333 Archibald, Lord Douglas led the Scottish army in a feint towards Bamburgh in the hopes of drawing the English away from Berwick which they were besieging. It failed, and the Scots had little alternative but to march directly to the aid of the beleaguered garrison. This particular siege of Berwick was ruthless. The castellan gave his two young sons to Edward III as hostages. Edward had inherited his grandfather's ruthless streak; he executed the young boys with neither compunction or compassion. The Scottish army clashed with the English at Halidon Hill and was routed. Berwick was forced to surrender.

Bamburgh Castle c1960 B547025

Bamburgh also holds the distinction of being the first castle to be breached by gunfire. During the Wars of the Roses Bamburgh was besieged by the Yorkists in 1461 and again in 1464. The latter siege was conducted by Edward IV, who deployed two large cannon. However it should be pointed out that the garrison was already on the point of surrendering, having eaten the last of their horses.

Seahouses, The Harbour c1936 S521027

Originally known as North Sunderland, Seahouses prospered on fishing, and for a while lime burning. After the trade finished in the 1860s some pre-1825 kiln arches on the quayside saw service as fishermen's stores.

SEAHOUSES, THE HARBOUR c1955 S521135
As well as fishing, boat trips to the Farne Islands start from here. In AD676 St Cuthbert chose to live in seclusion on Inner Farne and remained there for eight years until his elevation to bishop. Cuthbert was away from the island for only two years before he chose to return, dying a few months later.

SEAHOUSES, THE HARBOUR c1955 S521059
The early harbour, built in the 1780s of red and grey sandstone, now forms the inner harbour. In the 1880s the harbour was enlarged with new piers and a breakwater. There were schemes to turn Seahouses into one of the principal fishing ports in the north-east, and on the strength of this the privately-sponsored North Sunderland Light Railway was constructed. The line linked Seahouses to the North Eastern Railway at Chathill.

EMBLETON, FRONT STREET c1960 E150043
Around the time this picture was taken both Embleton and Beadnell were becoming popular with tourists; Beadnell in particular was being developed for caravan holidays. One of the attractions at Embleton is its golf course, once only 9 holes but now the full 18. In the early years following the end of the Great War Embleton was one of the Northumberland courses where golfers could get a round on Sundays.

BEADNELL, THE HARBOUR c1955 B550036
Disused lime kilns dominate the small harbour. They were built in 1798 by Richard Pringle for John Wood of Beadnell Hall, and it was Wood who also extended the harbour for the export of lime and coal. The kilns are now owned by the National Trust.

BEADNELL, THE HARBOUR c1955 B550008

Here we see traditional Northumbrian inshore fishing cobles at Beadnell. The village still sees some crab and lobster fishing, and Beadnell Bay is excellent for sailing.

BEADNELL, THE CRASTER ARMS AND THE CHURCH c1955 B550039

The church, dedicated to St Ebba, was built around 1740 and enlarged in 1792 when the tower and spire were also added. The unusual octagonal screen around the base of the spire was added later in 1860. The pub has an 18th-century frontage, but is based on an earlier tower house. It features the coat of arms of the Craster family.

CRASTER

Dunstanburgh Castle c1960 C352065

Dunstanburgh is the largest castle in Northumberland, built by Thomas, Earl of Lancaster; the licence to crenellate was granted shortly after the loss of Berwick to the Scots. The grandson of Henry III, Thomas was considered to be one of the greatest noblemen of his day. He was, however, fearful for the future. He had played a major role in the downfall of Piers Gaveston, Edward II's favourite and lover; Dunstanburgh was as much for his own protection as it was a defence against the Scots. In 1322, whilst on his way to Dunstanburgh, Thomas was captured by Edward's troops at Boroughbridge and later executed. The castle then became a royal fortress.

CRASTER, THE HARBOUR c1950 C352033
Though a fishing village since the 17th century, there was no harbour at Craster until the 20th century. It was paid for by the Craster family and built between 1906 and 1910 as a memorial to a member of the family, who appears to have died in Tibet.

CRASTER, THE VILLAGE c1960 C352052
Craster oak-smoked kippers are considered to be the best in England, and anyone paying a visit to the village really should not leave without buying some. Local boats still fish for crab and lobster, though fish for the kipper industry is brought in from North Shields.

ALNMOUTH, GENERAL VIEW C1965 A222015

Six miles south of Craster, the seaside resort of Alnmouth was once the port for Alnwick. From the 12th century until Christmas Day 1806, large amounts of grain were shipped out of Alnmouth, and timber, slate, and later guano, were imported through it. Then disaster struck. A storm changed the course of the Aln, which in turn led to the silting up of the harbour. Evidence to the power of the storm can still be seen to the south of the village. There, standing alone amid the fields, is a guano shed; the Aln once flowed past it.

ALNMOUTH, MARINE DRIVE FROM THE LINKS c1965 A222021

As a resort Alnmouth was noted for its excellent golf links, said to be one of the oldest in England. In the early 1920s the green fee on the 18-hole course was 2s 6d; Alnmouth was one of only a handful of Northumberland courses to welcome members of the Ladies Golf Union.

ALNMOUTH, NORTHUMBERLAND STREET c1950 A222030

Northumberland Street runs along the spine of the spur on which the town is built. After the harbour had become unusable, a number of warehouses and granaries were redeveloped. The Marine House Hotel was built as a granary and later converted into a vicarage. Hindmarsh Hall is an 18th-century granary, gothicized in the 19th century.

Alnmouth, The Beach c1965 A222029

For years Alnmouth has been noted for its sands; many of these holidaymakers would have taken a constitutional walking along the beach to Warkworth Castle. Had you been standing on the beach on a certain day in 1779, you might have seen the American warship 'Bonhomme Richard', commanded by John Paul Jones, cruising just off the mouth of the Aln. Jones fired his 68 lb carronade at the old church, but missed. The cannon ball hit the ground and bounced along before smashing into the end of a farmhouse.

Amble, The Beach c1965 A225048

Amble was little more than a hamlet until the construction of Warkworth Harbour in the late 1830s. Amble became a centre for coal exports, and was served by a branch line of the North Eastern Railway. Today it is hard to imagine that in 1913 there were 120 coalmines in Northumberland alone, and 67 when the NCB was formed in 1947. Coal exports ceased in 1969, the same year that the railway line was closed.

Amble, The Pier c1965 A225053

Before the Great War, Amble was one of Northumberland's smaller fishing ports; the biggest catches tended to be landed at North Shields, Blyth and Newbiggin. In 1912 the combined catch of white fish landed at Northumberland ports was 467,328 cwts. This did not include mackerel, crabs, lobsters and periwinkles.

AMBLE, HIGH STREET c1965 A225033
When this picture was taken it is unlikely that anyone thought that the port had only a few years left. In 1846 coal exported from the Tyne ports was just over 3,250,000 tonnes. By 1894 exports had risen to over 12 million tonnes, and by 1911 had topped 20 million tonnes.

AMBLE, QUEEN STREET c1960 A225037
The street was developed during the 1830s as the town grew in response to the construction of the harbour for the export of coal. On Queen Street are the scant remains of the medieval manor house that once belonged to Tynemouth Priory: a fragment of wall and a 15th-century window.

CRESSWELL TOWER c1955 C460009

Looking out over Druridge Bay, the rectangular three-storey tower of the late 14th to early 15th centuries takes its name from the Cresswell family. The ground floor is barrel-vaulted and the entrance is on the north side at first floor level, both typical defensive measures in tower houses on both sides of the Border. The embattled parapet is an 18th-century addition belonging to the time when a new house was built onto the north side. The house was later demolished, and all that remains is the pedimented doorway on the right of the picture. This now forms part of a field wall.

NEWBIGGIN-BY-THE-SEA, FRONT STREET c1955 N76003

A small resort, and former home to a large inshore fishing fleet, Newbiggin, even in 1955, had seen better days. Many Northumberland resorts are famed for the quality of their sands, but alas for Newbiggin - both pollution and wave action have taken their toll.

SEATON SLUICE, THE HARBOUR c1955 S523010
Seaton Sluice is a small natural harbour once known as Hartley Harbour. A problem with silting was tackled by Sir Ralph Delaval in the early 1670s. He built a pier and arranged for sea water to be trapped behind a sluice at each high tide. At low tide the sluice was opened and the harbour flushed: hence Seaton Sluice.

WHITLEY BAY, SOUTH LOWER PROMENADE c1955 W246007
It was the coming of the railway that transformed Whitley Bay into a resort and commuter country. Like Blackpool, Whitley Bay became a popular destination for holiday-makers from Glasgow, and it also prospered as a tripper resort for the people of Tyneside. Special low fares after 6.00pm brought in evening visitors by the hundreds. The railway also turned Whitley Bay into commuter country for those who could afford to escape the grime of Newcastle.

WHITLEY BAY, SPANISH CITY c1955 W246001
Spanish City was built in ferro-concrete between 1908 and 1910 as a theatre and amusement arcade for Whitley Pleasure Gardens Ltd. The dome is thought to be one of the earliest ferro-concrete domes in Britain.

CULLERCOATS, FISHERMEN'S COTTAGES c1955 C283006
A coal port in the 17th century, and a 'des res' for the well-heeled of Newcastle from the late 19th century onwards, Cullercoats was also a noted fishing community. From the doors of these cottages fisherwives in their distinctive costume sold fish. A similar situation used to exist at Newhaven, near Edinburgh. There, the women wore a costume that reflected their Dutch and Scandinavian origins. They also had their own cries when selling fish; 'Caller Herrin' for fresh herrings; 'Caller Ou' for fresh oysters.

Gosforth, High Street 1956 G125008

Though only a couple of miles to the north of Newcastle, Gosforth had a character and identity of its own. Every year during the last week in June the town would be packed with people for Race Week and the running of the Northumberland Plate. In 1947 over 57,000 punters flocked to Newcastle Races on Plate Day to see the first running of the race since 1939. The winner was Culrain by three-quarters of a length from Procne and Find The Lady.

WALLSEND, TOWN HALL 1951 W168002
The Town Hall with its round corner turret was designed by Liddell & Brown and built in 1907-08; the fire station in Lawson Street and the public baths were part of the same scheme. The Town Hall was later used for the North Tyneside District Offices.

WALLSEND, HIGH STREET c1955 W168001
Here we see a busy shopping scene. In 1955 a 14oz loaf cost 4d; streaky bacon was 2s 11d a pound; potatoes were 3d a pound; fish and chips 9d a portion; and eggs were 3s 11d a dozen.

NEWCASTLE, FROM RABBIT BANKS c1898 N16004

This photograph was taken from the Gateshead side of the river. Until 1800 Gateshead comprised little more than three main streets and was the northern end of the County Palatine of Durham. A third of the way along the old bridge over the Tyne were two blue stones; these marked the northern boundary of the Bishop of Durham's jurisdiction.

NESTLES FOOD

NEWCASTLE, THE QUAYSIDE 1896 N16320
In this picture the late 19th-century skyline of Newcastle is dominated by the 15th-century tower and spire of St Nicholas' Cathedral and the imposing bulk of the castle keep. Also featured are the Moot Hall, built 1810-12, and the much older Guildhall, which was completely rebuilt by Robert Trollop in 1655-58 and extended by John Dobson.

NEWCASTLE, THE QUAYSIDE 1928 N16316
The arrival of a ship for loading or unloading brought the Quayside to life. The steam lorry belonging to brewers William McEwan & Co might be a clue to the cargo. McEwans was founded in 1856 at the Fountain Brewery, Edinburgh; the beers were sold under two names, McEwans or Younger, depending on the area. This means that McEwan 80/- is the same as Younger IPA and McEwan 70/- is identical to Younger Scotch Bitter.

E.W. YOUNGER & Co L^TD
TRANSPORT SPECIALISTS.
Albion
XN·5270

NEWCASTLE, THE SWING BRIDGE 1890 N16018
When the late 18th-century bridge over the Tyne was demolished in the 1870s to make way for the Swing Bridge, traces of an earlier medieval bridge (destroyed by flood in 1771) and a Roman bridge were discovered. The Swing Bridge cost £288,000 to build. It has an overall length of 560ft; the swing section is 281ft, giving two navigable channels each 104ft wide. The superstructure was designed and built by Sir W G Armstrong at Elswick and was floated into place.

NEWCASTLE, THE SANDHILL 1894 N16019
By this time the former house of banker Aubone Surtees had become the warehouse of J W Newton & Co. On the night of 18th November 1772, Bessy Surtees climbed down a ladder from one of the windows and into the arms of her lover John Scott. The couple then fled across the Scottish border and were married at Blackshiels, Midlothian. Scott later became Lord Chancellor of England.

NEWCASTLE, THE CASTLE 1901 N16022

In 1812 the castle was bought by the Corporation, and it was after this date that the corner turrets and battlements were added to the keep. Also in the picture is the Black Gate, originally constructed in 1247 when the castle's defences were upgraded. The house on the top of the gate is a much later addition.

W. BRENNAN
CIGAR
MERCHANT

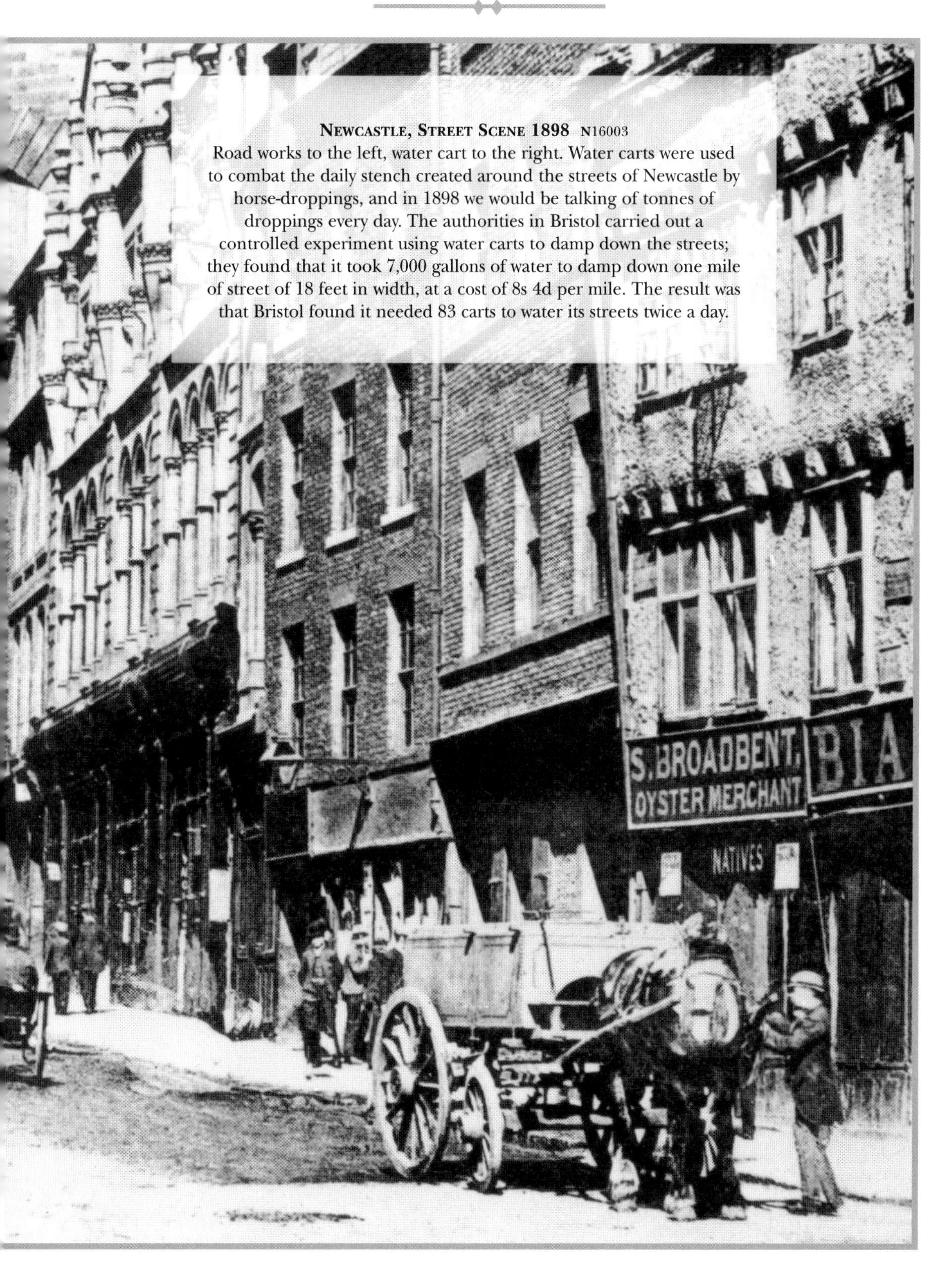

Newcastle, Street Scene 1898 N16003
Road works to the left, water cart to the right. Water carts were used to combat the daily stench created around the streets of Newcastle by horse-droppings, and in 1898 we would be talking of tonnes of droppings every day. The authorities in Bristol carried out a controlled experiment using water carts to damp down the streets; they found that it took 7,000 gallons of water to damp down one mile of street of 18 feet in width, at a cost of 8s 4d per mile. The result was that Bristol found it needed 83 carts to water its streets twice a day.

NEWCASTLE, NEVILLE STREET C1901 N16002
This is a classic view of Neville Street, with the entrance to the Central Station on the left and St Mary's Roman Catholic Church in the background. The awning in the foreground is the entrance to the Station Hotel, which was well spoken of in the tour guides of the time. Here, rooms cost 4s a night and dinner 3s 6d; the County Hotel across the street had a similar tariff, as did the nearby Metropole.

NEWCASTLE, GREY STREET 1890 N16017
This view looks towards the Grey Monument. On the right is the Norfolk Commercial Hotel and the Theatre Royal; its pediment bearing the royal arms is supported by six Corinthian columns. The theatre was bought by the local authority in 1971 after the then owners, Howard & Wyndhams, announced that they were going to turn it into a bingo hall. The authority had made a commitment to maintain live theatre in Newcastle. Proposals ranged from building a new theatre to supporting the recently opened University Theatre off the Haymarket.

NEWCASTLE, GREY STREET 1900 N16021
Grey Street is to the left, Grainger Street to the right. Between them Richard Grainger, John Dobson and John Clayton were responsible for much of the centre of Newcastle. Grainger and Dobson supplied the architectural talent, and Clayton the money and the influence. Here, partially hidden by the column of the Grey Monument, is Grainger's Central Exchange, a triangular-shaped block with each of the three points finished by domes. Have you spotted the net full of balls above the entrance to Murton's sports shop?

NEWCASTLE, GRAINGER STREET 1900 N16314
Here we see Grainger Street before work began on electrification of the street tramway. This is a busy picture - there are lots of things going on, and it might be worth getting the magnifying-glass out. Note the young lad on the right; he has no shoes. Over on the left outside Harkers are two large hampers on a barrow. Harkers might be getting a visit from a salesman. It was common practice at this time for commercial travellers to carry their samples in hampers. They travelled to the big cities by train, hiring a barrow and boy to trundle along behind them from one call to another.

CORBRIDGE, MARKET PLACE c1955 C459016

Corbridge is a small town with a traumatic history. Situated on one of the main crossing points of the Tyne, Corbridge was occupied by the Scots in 1138 and burnt by them on at least three occasions; by William Wallace in 1296; by the Bruce in 1312; and by David II in 1346. There was a time when Corbridge held a weekly market, but this petered out as the town declined following the Civil War.

Corbridge, Main Street c1955 C459015

The building facing our cameraman is Monksholme, built in the early 17th century as an inn; it has genuine attic dormers, and was restored in 1891. Across the road to the left stands Low Hall. This building is thought to be a late 13th- to early 14th-century hall that was raised to a pele-tower during the 15th century. A major extension was added to the rear of the building during the 19th century.

Corbridge, The Angel Inn c1955 C459006

The 17th-century Angel Inn stands at the east end of Middle Street and the start of Main Street, and is one of a number of interesting buildings around the area. In the churchyard stands a fortified vicarage built in 1318, and Heron House dates from 1700. To the south-west of the town stands the ruined Dilston Hall, home of the Earls of Derwentwater, the last of whom was executed for his role in the Jacobite rebellion of 1715.

HEXHAM, BEAUMONT STREET c1965 H80095

Beaumont Street is named after the family of Viscount Allendale; here stands the great Abbey Church of St Andrew that makes Hexham important. The first church at Hexham was founded by St Wilfred on land given to him in AD674 by Queen Ethelreda of Northumbria. The present Abbey dates from the 12th to the 15th centuries, though the crypt of St Wilfred's original church remains, as does his cut-out square stone seat (the Frith Stool). The east end of the Abbey was rebuilt in 1858, and the nave in the early 20th century.

Acomb, The Village c1955 A250007
Acomb was once a centre for the lead-mining industry. An old building dating from 1730 is still known as the barracks, a name said to derive from its use as a lodging house for lead miners.

Acomb, Garden House c1955 A250001
In the 1950s Acomb boasted a number of 18th-century buildings. Tynevale House was built in 1754, Town Head in 1796, and the Miners Arms in 1750. Acomb House, to the south of the village square, was built in the 1730s, though it is thought to incorporate the remnants of an earlier house.

ACOMB, THE OLD MILL c1955 A250002
The mill is just south of the village on the Birkey Burn. The miller's house is dated 1728, and the three-storey mill building is also 18th-century. Though normally powered by water, the mill could operate in conjunction with a nearby windmill if there was insufficient water in the burn. Modernisation came during the 19th century when the mill was equipped with a steam engine.

BELTINGHAM, RIDLEY HALL c1950 B829021
Situated to the east of Beltingham, Ridley Hall was rebuilt in the 1890s in a neo-Tudor style. The octagonal tower stands at the south-west corner: the architect, Horatio Adamson, drew inspiration from Carnarfon Castle as the basis for his design.

HALTWHISTLE, MAIN STREET c1960 H344046
The market town of Haltwhistle straddles the present-day A69 a few miles from the border with Cumbria. Featured here is the Red Lion Hotel, a rare example of an urban tower house built for defence against Scots and Border raiders, though it does not have a vaulted basement.

GREENHEAD, THE VILLAGE C1955 G310001
The church, dedicated to St Cuthbert, was designed by John Dobson and built between 1826 and 1828. It consisted of an aisleless nave and a narrow west tower with an octagonal spire; the chancel was added in 1900. About one mile to the north-west is the bastle house of Low Old Shield, one of many fortified farmhouses built during the days of the Border raids.

GILSLAND, THE ROMAN WALL 1924 76661
Here we see a section of Hadrian's Wall near the village of Gilsland. 73 miles long, with seventeen forts, mile-castles and turrets, the wall was one of a number of linear defences built to designate the territorial limits of the Roman empire. Additional flank defences were constructed along the Solway shore as far as present-day Whitehaven. The presence of garrisons stimulated civilian settlement, agriculture and local industry.

GILSLAND

The Village c1950 G211012

Poltross Burn, which flows through the middle of the village, marks the border between Northumberland and Cumbria. The village enjoyed a brief career as a spa, and it was here that Walter Scott first met his future wife Charlotte Carpenter. Some years later the couple were revisiting the spa when the expected invasion by Napoleon was signalled throughout much of the North by the lighting of beacons. Scott hurried back to Scotland to enlist, covering more than a hundred miles in less than twenty-four hours only to find that it had been a false alarm.

ETAL, THE VILLAGE c1955 E151003
Despite the fact that they were supposed to be on the same side when it came to defending the Borders, the Herons of Ford and the Manners of Etal did not always see eye-to-eye. In January 1428 a quarrel between William Heron (the younger) and John Manners culminated in a pitched battle between their armed retainers at Etal. Heron was butchered in the traditional Border fashion; the only other fatality was one Robert Atkinson. A royal commission was appointed to investigate the killing, and it ended with Manners having to go to Newcastle and submit. He was ordered to have 500 masses sung within a year for Heron's soul and to pay his widow 250 marks.

Ford Castle c1950 F207007

Along with Etal, Ford Castle once formed a second line of defence against the Scots; the front line consisted of the fortresses at Wark, Berwick and Norham. Ford was built as a manor house by William Heron in 1338, but it was quickly raised in status to a castle. By 1367 Ford had been integrated into English defence planning for the North. The present castle dates mainly from the 1860s, though the north and south-west towers are original.

Ford, The Blacksmith's Workshop c1955 F207001

Just six miles from the Borde, the village of Ford sits on gently rising ground on the right bank of the Till. The parish, which included Etal, Kimmerston, Hetherslaw and Crookham, suffered much during the wars with Scotland. In the 1340s the damage was so great that the parish sought exemption from taxation because crops and goods had been destroyed and livestock taken. There was also an old custom that allowed tenants to pay only half-rents following war with the Scots.

BELFORD, THE CROSS AND MAIN ROAD c1950 B553009
Belford is just one of many places in Northumberland that suffered during the cross-border raids that were a feature of life in the North for several centuries. It is possible that the village was destroyed on more than one occasion. In 1639, about thirty years after the Border raiders and reivers had been ruthlessly suppressed by James II, Belford was still described as 'the most miserable, beggarly town, or town of sods, that ever was made...' The people were living in hovels roofed with sod or heather.

BELFORD, THE SQUARE c1965 B553071
The small market town of Belford was once a coaching stop for travellers on the Great North Road. The Blue Bell Hotel dates from the 18th century and is unusual in that it is built of brick; all the other older buildings are of ashlar.

BELFORD, ST MARY'S CHURCH c1955 B553011
Though St Mary's contains a Norman chancel arch, much of the building dates from John Dobson's restoration of 1828-29. Dobson restored the chancel and nave and added a north aisle and the west tower. A porch was added in 1844. The next major alteration came in 1965, when the north gallery was blocked off to form a village hall.

Glanton, The Village c1950 G212004

Consisting of little more than one long street running east to west, Glanton enjoyed a reputation for the healing properties of the water from the Keppin or Keppie Well situated behind the old school house. The custom carried out during the summer months was for parents to wrap their weakly offspring in blankets and place them under the well spout. The well's name is derived from the days when villagers would draw water which was then kept in pails, jugs or skeels.

Glanton, The Village c1950 G212007

Glanton stands on a ridge about two miles north of Whittingham and nine miles west-by-north of Alnwick. In the reign of King John it was held by William de Flammavill; by the middle of the 13th century it had been divided between several landowners.

Alnwick, The Hotspur Gate c1955 A223006

Guarding the road from the south, the Hotspur Gate was built in 1450; a licence to fortify the Border town of Alnwick had been granted in 1434. Above the entrance there is a much-decayed lion rampant, emblem of the Percy family, and above that are corbels that once carried a machicolation to enhance the defensive capability of the flanking projections.

ALNWICK

The Lion Monument c1955 A223016

The first thing that greets travellers arriving from the south is the Percy Tenantry Column, known locally as the Farmers' Folly. It was built in 1816, and the story most often told is that it was erected by the duke's tenant farmers in thanks for having their rents remitted during a period of agricultural depression. The story goes on that the duke, surprised that his tenants could afford such a memorial, immediately put their rents up. The truth is that it was erected by the members of the Percy Tenantry Volunteers, a unit raised by the duke for home defence during the Napoleonic Wars.

ALNWICK, THE WHITE SWAN c1955 A223007

The White Swan stands on the north side of Bondgate Within. The frontage is mid 19th-century, but the real gem is inside. The 59ft x 63ft Olympic Room is comprised of fittings salvaged from the 'Titanic's' sister ship 'Olympic' which was broken up at Jarrow in the 1930s.

Alnwick, Bondgate Hill c1955 A223020
Here we see Bondgate with its famous slope of cobbles. The buildings on the right are mainly late 18th- and early 19th-century. Just coming into the picture at left is the local branch of Lloyds, built around 1910 to the designs of local architect George Reavell. Beyond Lloyds is Barclays, which incorporates an 18th-century house.

Alnwick, Bondgate and Market Place c1955 A223017
This photograph was taken from Bondgate Within. In the centre, partially hidden by trees, is the Northumberland Hall, built in 1826 by the third Duke to provide the town with an assembly rooms. By the mid-1960s the open arcaded ground floor was being used for shops, and the assembly rooms above for Bingo.

Alnwick Castle c1955 A223010
The 11th-century castle was extended by the Percy family following its purchase by them in 1309. The shell keep was rebuilt by Henry de Percy, and the second Earl is thought to have built the barbican and gatehouse around 1440. As we can see here, two square towers flank the archway, and these are in turn supported by a pair of octagonal towers. Between the two sets of towers there was once a moat spanned by a drawbridge.

Alnwick Castle c1955 A223014
One of the five great fortresses of Northumberland, Alnwick fell into ruins owing in part to the fate of the Percy family and the destruction wreaked by Cromwell's troops. On the death of the eleventh Earl in 1670 the earldom became extinct. An 18th-century female descendant of the last earl married Sir Hugh Smithson, who changed his name to Percy and was created Earl of Northumberland in 1750 and first Duke of Northumberland in 1766. It was this Hugh Percy who set about restoring Alnwick to its former glory, commissioning Robert Adam to supervise the decoration and Capability Brown to lay out the grounds. Further alterations and rebuilding was carried out during the 19th century.

Shilbottle, The Farrier's Arms 1955 S518003

Shilbottle

The Farrier's Arms 1955

Locals from the solid-looking Farrier's Arms pose for the camera. The other solid building in the village was the old vicarage, a former much-altered pele-tower with a barrel-vaulted ground floor. In 1955 the village also boasted a number of 18th-century cottages.

Rothbury

The Queen's Head c1955

In the early 19th century the Border town of Rothbury enjoyed a reputation as a health resort, where during the summer season visitors could 'drink goat's whey and enjoy the salubrious air of the place'. There was also horse racing on Rothbury Haugh, which attracted people from throughout Coquetdale. But the town owes much of its growth to the coming of the railway and the nearby Armstrong estate of Cragside. Lord Armstrong began building Cragside in the 1860s; he also built almshouses in the town (1896) as well as the Addycombe cottages (1873) for retired staff from his estate.

Rothbury, The Queen's Head c1955 R360047

Felton, St Michael's Church c1955 F153002

The roofs of the nave and south aisle are so low that a first glance at St Michael's often leaves visitors thinking that the building is semi-derelict. The chancel, with its high-pitched roof, dates from the early 13th century, though some parts of the church are thought to be 12th-century. The aisles were added in the 14th century and a chantry endowed in 1331. During the 19th century the north aisle was extended, a vestry built and the east end rebuilt.

Felton, The Old Bridge c1955 F153028

Felton stands on the north bank of the Coquet, and it was here that the Great North Road once crossed the river by way of the old bridge featured in the picture. The bridge, complete with pedestrian refuges, is thought to be 15th-century: some of the houses facing the bridge date from the early 17th to early 19th centuries.

ASHINGTON, MILBURN ROAD c1960 A224022
Ashington is just one of hundreds of places in England that owes its existence to the age of industrialisation. Before the area was opened up for coal mining Ashington was but a farm; it was the Ashington Coal Co who developed the town, building 300 houses for pitmen and their families.

HIRST PARK

MAYNARDS

MORPETH, BRIDGE STREET c1965 M251069
This is the main shopping street between the Market Place and New Bridge. On the right is the Black Bull Hotel, noted for its two-storey bow window which projects into the street. Also here, where numbers 26-32 now stand, was once the gaol and the Governor's House.

MORPETH, FROM THE OLD BRIDGE c1965 M251050
This photograph was taken from the old footbridge, of which only the central pier and abutments remain; the cast iron section was added in 1869. The building in the centre of the picture with the bellcote is The Chantry; it is thought to have been founded by Robert of Morpeth around 1296. The Chantry was partially remodelled in the 1730s and underwent a sympathetic restoration in 1980. Over on the right is the Telford Bridge of 1829-31 designed by John Dobson.

BEDLINGTON, THE MARKET PLACE c1965 B551007
The obelisk is in fact an 18th-century market cross. The town grew during the 1840s with the sinking of the first coal mine in the locality. Like Durham, Bedlington became known for its annual Miners' Gala, when there were brass bands, Lodge banners, speeches, and plenty to drink.

Bedlington, Front Street East c1960 B551006

Bedlington was once the capital of Bedlingtonshire, and as a part of the County Palatine of Durham belonged to the Bishops of Durham until 1844. The parish church is dedicated to St Cuthbert in memory of a night in 1069 when monks escaping from Durham with the saint's remains sheltered here on their way to Holy Island to be out of reach of the Normans.

BEDLINGTON, FRONT STREET WEST c1960 B551012

Front Street is a long wide high street that leads down to the River Blyth. The town is also the birthplace of Daniel Gooch; having served his apprenticeship at Robert Stephenson's works, he was only 21 years old when he was appointed Locomotive Superintendent of the Great Western Railway. Gooch was later knighted and became Chairman of the GWR in 1865.

BELSAY, THE VILLAGE c1955 B554007

The old village, which consisted of about eighteen houses, lay to the south-west of Belsay Castle - or rather it did until the early 19th century, when Sir Charles Monck had it demolished and moved to the main road.

Belsay, The Village c1955 B554008

The new village was in fact one long terraced row featuring an arcaded ground floor; this was a reflection of Sir Charles Monck's taste for things Italian. Sir Charles travelled widely; he took his bride off on a honeymoon that lasted two years, much of it spent exploring Germany, Italy and Greece.

Belsay

The Old Castle c1955 B554001

Built of honey-coloured sandstone, the old castle is in fact a 14th-century L-plan tower house built by the de Middleton family. There are four corner turrets, each with rounded bartizans corbelled out, and the parapet has machicolations; this was an overhang that allowed defenders to drop missiles on the heads of uninvited guests. It is not known if Belsay ever had a curtain wall, or if there were other buildings associated with it. The manor house extension was added in 1614. In 1807 Sir Charles Monck abandoned the old castle for a new residence, Belsay Hall. Built in the Doric style, the Hall was considered an architectural novelty of the day.

Seaton Delaval, The Hall c1965 S522007
Seven miles north of Tynemouth, the Hall was designed by Sir John Vanbrugh, and completed for Admiral George Delaval in 1707. Over the years the Hall has experienced its share of misfortune. The west wing was destroyed by fire in May 1752, though it was rebuilt to Vanburgh's original designs. In January 1822 the central block was badly damaged by fire; though time and money was spent reroofing it, it remained uninhabitable.

Bellingham, Market Place c1960 B552046
Bellingham straddles the B6320 that winds its way from the near Hadrian's Wall to Otterburn. The town is considered the gateway to the moors and forests of the Northumberland National Park, and the Pennine Way also passes through the town. The town has not always been peaceful: like many others in this part of the country it suffered at the hands of the Borderers, who raided and reived until they were finally suppressed in the early 17th century by James II.

BELLINGHAM, HIGH STREET c1960 B552019

BELLINGHAM
High Street c1960
On the left is the Town Hall with its unusual lead-sheathed clock turret. The town is also noted for its late 19th-century iron railings and for St Cuthbert's Church, which has a type of roof unusual in Northumberland. The roof is of single and double thickness stone slabs laid alternately down the roof pitch, possibly as a defence against raiders who often used fire when attacking buildings; at least two previous wooden roofs are known to have been destroyed by fire.

ALLENDALE
Main Road c1955
Once the market town for Northumberland's principal lead-mining area, Allendale Town also lays claim to be at the geographical centre of the UK. The lead-mines are long gone; by the 1950s the town's economy was centred upon hill farming and a growing tourist trade.

ALLENDALE, MAIN ROAD c1955 A102061

Allendale, The Dale Hotel and the Square c1955 A102015

A legacy from Allendale's lead-mining and market town days was that it was well provided with hotels, like the ivy-clad Dale Hotel seen here, as well as a number of quality public houses. In 1998 Allendale had two entries in the Good Beer Guide: the Golden Lion, and the King's Head Hotel. Both serve guest beers, but it is to the Golden Lion that we go for Butterknowle Conciliation, and the to the King's Head for Jennings Cumberland.

Allendale, The Hotspur Hotel c1960 A102134

Allendale appears almost deserted in this picture, so it cannot be New Year's Eve. That's the day when people come from all over Northumberland to watch Allendale's special celebrations, which are thought to be Norse in origin. Twenty-four men, accompanied by a band, march round the town, their faces blackened, carrying barrels of blazing tar above their heads. The barrels finish up on a bonfire, everyone has a good time, and come midnight the custom of first-footing is actively pursued.

ALLENDALE, STREET SCENE c1960 A102115
In the centre background, partially hidden by trees, is the Hitherlea; the Hotspur Hotel is on the left hand side of the picture, but it is totally obscured.

ALLENHEADS, ROPEHAUGH c1965 A221018
Situated at the head of the valley of the East Allen, Allenheads was an important centre for the lead-mining industry from the late 18th to the mid 19th century; the mines here produced around 14 per cent of the country's total output. The influx of mine workers brought with it an expansion of the village. New Houses was built in 1788, and Fawside Green and Dudley Place in 1790. Also dating from 1790 is Iceton House, which was once the pay office. There were even workings under the village itself, which were reached by way of a spiral incline.

ALLENHEADS, SLAG HILL COTTAGES c1965 A221020
The somewhat interestingly named hamlet of Dirt Pot lies just one mile north of Allenheads. It was here, during the heyday of the lead mining industry, that the lead was smelted in a mill, though the only intact remnant today is the peat house. On the Coalcleugh road from Dirt Pot was the Slag Hill limekiln, which consisted of two elliptical-plan kiln pots. Most of the cottages and small holdings were originally built for mine workers.

BLANCHLAND, THE VILLAGE c1950 B555004
To the north-east of Allenheads beyond Nookton Fell lies the village of Blanchland. It was here in 1165 that an Abbey Church was founded by the Praemonstratensian Order of monks. The Abbey featured more than once in the turbulent history of the North. A Scots raiding force attempting to find the Abbey had managed to get itself lost in a thick mist that had descended over the area. Thinking themselves delivered from the heathens, the brothers rang the Abbey bells in celebration. Guided by the bells, the Scots fell on the abbey which they then ransacked and burnt, killing a number of monks in the process.

BLANCHLAND, THE VILLAGE c1950 B555010
This view features the church of St Mary the Virgin. It is unusual in that it is an L-plan building incorporating the Abbey chancel, crossing and north transept with its 13th-century tower and 14th-century belfry. Also featured is the bridge over the Derwent by which visitors from the south enter the village. Those coming from the north pass under the Abbey's embattled 15th-century gatehouse.

Blanchland, The Village c1950 B555045
The Abbey was dissolved in 1539. Its lands were sold to John Bellow and John Bloxham, though they later passed into the hands of the Forsters of Bamburgh. Forced to sell for financial reasons, Tom and Dorothy Forster sold the village to Lord Crewe, Bishop of Durham, and their aunt's husband.

Blanchland, Bay Bridge Road c1950 B555013
The centre of the village dates from the restoration and repairs begun in 1752 by Lord Crewe's trustees. The village square appears to be sited on the L-shaped outer court of the Abbey, where the barns, storehouses and workshops would once have stood. Slag found under houses on the west side might indicate that the Abbey carried out some lead or silver smelting.

RYTON, MAIN ROAD c1960 R88005
When this picture was taken, Ryton was a pit village in County Durham with no less than five working pits in the immediate vicinity. Now a part of Tyne & Wear, Ryton, like a hundred or more other places, is pitless, though some light industry was attracted to the area. In the background is Holy Cross Church with its unusual broach spire.

Winlaton, The Village c1955 W248011

In 1690 Ambrose Crowley relocated his ironworks and workers from Sunderland to Winlanton and Swalwell. The works at Winlanton forged light tools, while that at Swalwell went in for heavier items, including cannon, anchors and chains. Crowley was ahead of his time; he built cottages for his workers and the community had the services of a doctor, schoolmaster and a parson. Crowley even established an arbitration court at which workers had representatives. The court settled all matters relating to pay and working conditions.

Whickham, Front Street c1955 W244001

Whickham was once an important economic asset to the prince bishops of Durham. In 1183 the Boldon Book refers to 'coalsmiths' at Sedgefield and Bishopwearmouth and to colliers at Escomb. Coal was being extracted at a profit from the Whickham and Gateshead area well before the end of the 13th century.

Whickham, The Highway c1955 W244008

Surviving accounts books for 1458-61, 1467-68, 1476-77, 1500 and 1509 show that the Whickham mines were contributing considerable revenues to the bishop. At the Reformation the Church's mines were confiscated by the Crown, who then offered them on 99-year leases to Newcastle merchants.

Monkton, The Village c1955 M319011

A part of Jarrow, Monkton has several interesting buildings. Bede House dates from the 17th century, Monkton Farmhouse from the 18th century, and Grange Farmhouse from the late 17th to early 18th centuries.

JARROW, GRANGE ROAD WEST c1955 J5004
Though a monastery was founded at Jarrow in AD681 by Benedict Biscop, the modern town owes its existence to Charles and George Palmer, who opened a shipyard here in 1851. The firm expanded rapidly, for it had its own coal mines, iron and steel making plant, and a marine engine works. The entire town was dependent on the yard, and when it went into liquidation in 1933 it left Jarrow with the highest unemployment rate in the country.

Jarrow, Grange Road West c1955 J5001
On the right is the Town Hall, built in 1902 to the designs of South Shields-based architect Fred Rennoldson. The area opposite the Town Hall was redeveloped in the late 1950s by the Arndale Property Trust in association with Shingler Risdon Associates. They built a two-storey shopping centre with two wide malls and covered arcades.

SOUTH SHIELDS, FREDERICK STREET c1906 S162002
During the first half of the 19th century a number of churches were built to meet the needs of South Shield's growing population. The Presbyterian Church, Frederick Street, was built in 1847; Holy Trinity, Laygate, was earlier, having been built in 1832-34 to the designs of Anthony Salvin. Both have since been demolished.

DOCK INDUSTRIAL CO-OPERATIVE

SOUTH SHIELDS, LAYGATE LANE 1900 S162001
Laygate Lane is one of a number of sturdy Victorian terraces in South Shields; many of them were built speculatively by developers as the town expanded thanks to the coal and alkali industries. In 1850 South Shields (including Westoe) became a municipal borough; Harton was added in 1901, and Cleadon Bank and Harton Village in 1921.

Whitburn
The Bank c1955

The village of Whitburn lies between South Shields and Sunderland. On the north side of the village green is this raised terrace. Two of the houses are Georgian; the half-timbered building is Whitburn House, which is dated 1869 and has a Perpendicular window from St John's Church, Newcastle.

Seaburn
Lower Promenade c1955

Along with Roker, Seaburn comprises what is in effect the seaside resort area of Sunderland; there have been times when the Cat and Dog steps have positively heaved with sunbathers. A popular attraction during the 1950s was the annual lights along the front and in Roker Park. Those who wanted an inexpensive holiday could book into Seaburn Camp, which even as late as 1960 looked like a German Stalag with flowerbeds.

Whitburn, The Bank c1955 W245013

Seaburn, Lower Promenade c1955 S340001

SUNDERLAND, ROKER PARK 1900 S263007
Time for a leisurely stroll through The Dene at Roker. It must be a hot sunny day - the children are wearing sunhats and a parasol is up.

SUNDERLAND, THE BRIDGES 1900 S263004
This picture gives us a good view of the old Wearmouth, or Sunderland, iron bridge. Beyond the dredger 'Titan' are several tugs, one of which belongs to Lambton Collieries, whose coal staithes can also be seen in the background.

SUNDERLAND, SHIPYARDS ON THE WEAR C1900 S263508
650 years of shipbuilding on the Wear came to an end with the closure of North East Shipbuilder's Southwick yard in 1989. Here, however, is a reminder of what it used to be like, with ships being fitted out on both sides of the river. Almost hidden in the centre background is one of the tugs belonging to Lambton Collieries, identifiable by its funnel colours of black with three red horizontal stripes. Around the time the picture was taken Lambton Collieries were sending between three and four million tonnes of coal a year to the Wear for shipment.

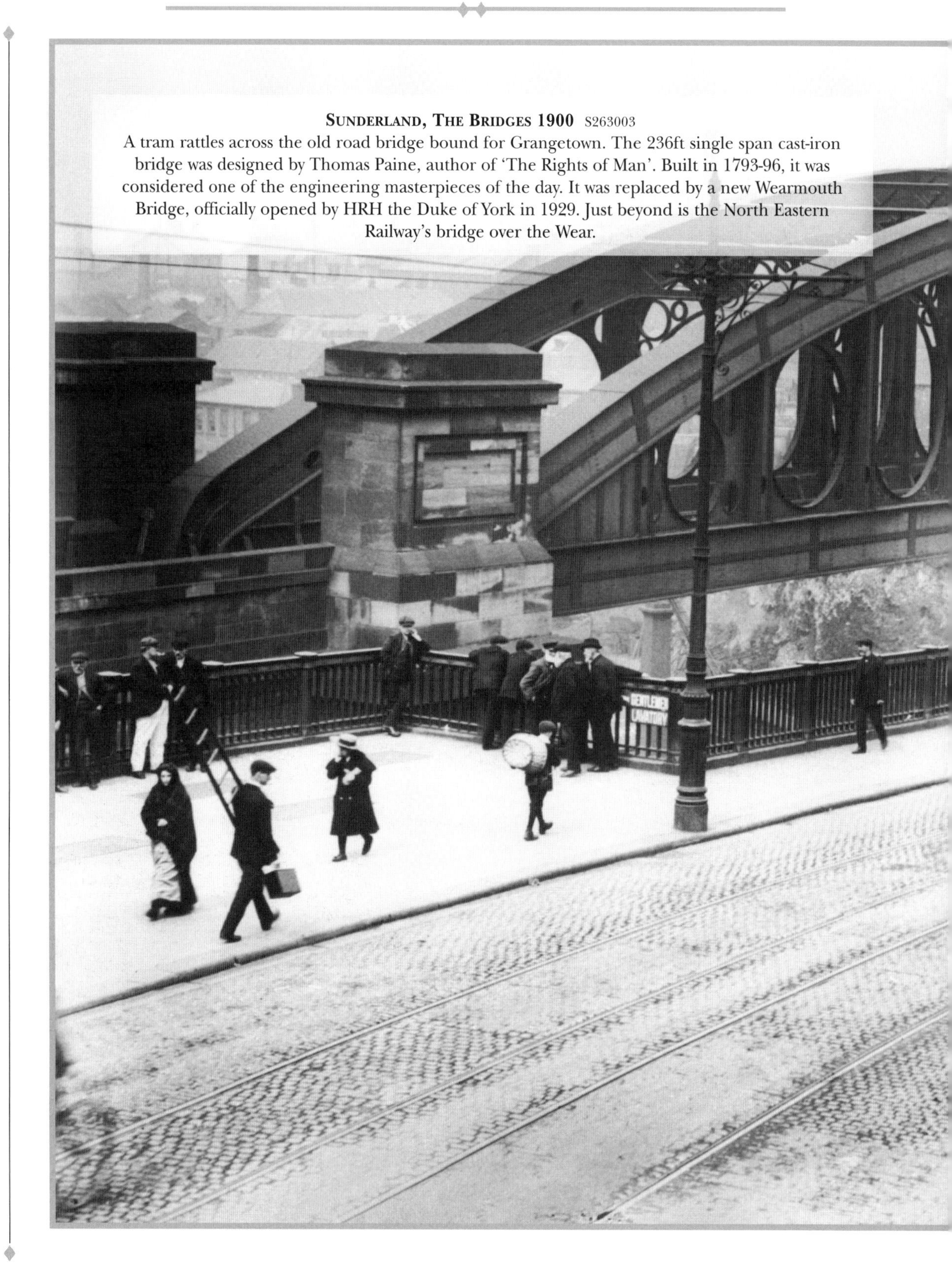

SUNDERLAND, THE BRIDGES 1900 S263003
A tram rattles across the old road bridge bound for Grangetown. The 236ft single span cast-iron bridge was designed by Thomas Paine, author of 'The Rights of Man'. Built in 1793-96, it was considered one of the engineering masterpieces of the day. It was replaced by a new Wearmouth Bridge, officially opened by HRH the Duke of York in 1929. Just beyond is the North Eastern Railway's bridge over the Wear.

SUNDERLAND, FAWCETT STREET 1890 S263001
This part of Sunderland developed into the commercial and civic heart of the town following the opening of Fawcett Street Station by the North Eastern Railway. In August 1879 both Fawcett Street and Hendon stations were closed on the opening of the new Central Station. In the picture is the Italianate Town Hall designed by Brightwen Binyon, which was demolished in 1971 after being replaced by a new civic centre at West Park.

SUNDERLAND, BOROUGH ROAD 1910 S263002
The Library and Museum was built in 1877-79 to the designs of J and T Tillman, a mixture of classical Roman and French mansard roofs. Despite its size, the building had only one storey.

SUNDERLAND, THE PARK c1900 S263509
This is Mowbray Park, created in the 1850s out of Bildon Hill and the old quarries on its north face. This picture shows the glass and cast-iron winter gardens built on the back of the Library and Museum. This ornate structure was destroyed by enemy bombing during the Second World War.

RYHOPE, THE VILLAGE c1960 R252021

In 1960 Ryhope was still very much a pit village, with its own colliery. In 1967 Ryhope, along with Silksworth, East Herrington, South Hylton, and Castletown, was incorporated into Sunderland.

WASHINGTON, MAIN STREET c1955 W242003

On the upper reaches of the Wear and once a part of County Durham, Washington was where William Doxford built his first ships before moving to Pallion in the 1870s. In 1964 the former colliery village became the hub of the newly created Washington New Town, the idea behind it being to attract commuters and overspill from both Tyneside and Wearside.

WASHINGTON, THE VILLAGE c1965 W242029

WASHINGTON
The Village c1965

This photograph was taken after the formation of Washington New Town. The New Town comprised Washington Village, Columbia, Fatfield, Mount Pleasant, Usworth, Donwell and Concord. By 1981 it comprised sixteen villages, 5610 acres, and had a population of about 50,000. Projections were for it to comprise eighteen villages and have a population of 68,000 by 1985.

WASHINGTON
The Village c1955

The two principal churches in the village at this time were the Roman Catholic Our Blessed Lady Immaculate, which dated from the late 1870s, and Holy Trinity, which had been rebuilt in the 1830s, extended in the 1880s, and given a bell tower in 1962.

WASHINGTON, THE VILLAGE c1955 W242005

Washington, Front Street 1955 W242010

At this time restoration work was under way at Washington Old Hall, home of the ancestors of US president George Washington. Among the interesting pieces of furniture at the Hall is a 17th-century Flemish-style bed, complete with a gun cupboard at its foot. In September 1955 the Colours of the Washington Greys (New York National Guard) were laid up at the Hall.

WEST BOLDON, ST NICHOLAS ROAD c1955 W554007
The area between the south bank of the Tyne and the north bank of the Wear was transformed during the 19th century as coal mines opened and communities grew around them. Nearby Boldon Colliery was sunk between 1866 and 1871, and it was substantially deepened under NCB ownership.

WEST BOLDON, THE VILLAGE c1955 W554009
Those were the days when the Red Lion still served Aitchie's Ales. Massive housing programmes started after the Second World War, which altered many of the pit villages. New estates contributed to an urban sprawl that has reduced rural areas and agricultural acreage. In some cases there is no longer any rural land left to separate one village from another.

Index

The Francis Frith Collection Titles

www.francisfrith.com

The Francis Frith Collection publishes over 100 new titles each year. A selection of those currently available is listed below. For latest catalogue please contact The Francis Frith Collection.

Town Books 96 pages, approximately 75 photos. ***County and Themed Books*** 128 pages, approximately 135 photos (unless specified). Pocket Albums are miniature editions of Frith local history books 128 pages, approximately 95 photos.

Accrington Old and New
Alderley Edge and Wilmslow
Amersham, Chesham and Rickmansworth
Andover
Around Abergavenny
Around Alton
Aylesbury
Barnstaple
Bedford
Bedfordshire
Berkshire Living Memories
Berkshire Pocket Album
Blackpool Pocket Album
Bognor Regis
Bournemouth
Bradford
Bridgend
Bridport
Brighton and Hove
Bristol
Buckinghamshire
Calne Living Memories
Camberley Pocket Album
Canterbury Cathedral
Cardiff Old and New
Chatham and the Medway Towns
Chelmsford
Chepstow Then and Now
Cheshire
Cheshire Living Memories
Chester
Chesterfield
Chigwell
Christchurch
Churches of East Cornwall
Clevedon
Clitheroe
Corby Living Memories
Cornish Coast
Cornwall Living Memories
Cotswold Living Memories
Cotswold Pocket Album
Coulsdon, Chipstead and Woodmanstern
County Durham
Cromer, Sheringham and Holt
Dartmoor Pocket Album
Derby
Derbyshire
Derbyshire Living Memories
Devon
Devon Churches
Dorchester
Dorset Coast Pocket Album
Dorset Living Memories
Dorset Villages
Down the Dart
Down the Severn
Down the Thames
Dunmow, Thaxted and Finchingfield
Durham
East Anglia Pocket Album
East Devon
East Grinstead
Edinburgh
Ely and The Fens
Essex Pocket Album
Essex Second Selection
Essex: The London Boroughs
Exeter
Exmoor
Falmouth
Farnborough, Fleet and Aldershot
Folkestone
Frome
Furness and Cartmel Peninsulas
Glamorgan
Glasgow
Glastonbury
Gloucester
Gloucestershire
Greater Manchester
Guildford
Hailsham
Hampshire
Harrogate
Hastings and Bexhill
Haywards Heath Living Memories
Heads of the Valleys
Heart of Lancashire Pocket Album
Helston
Herefordshire
Horsham
Humberside Pocket Album
Huntingdon, St Neots and St Ives
Hythe, Romney Marsh and Ashford
Ilfracombe
Ipswich Pocket Album
Isle of Wight
Isle of Wight Living Memories
King's Lynn
Kingston upon Thames
Lake District Pocket Album
Lancashire Living Memories
Lancashire Villages

Available from your local bookshop or from the publisher

The Francis Frith Collection Titles (continued)

Lancaster, Morecambe and Heysham Pocket Album
Leeds Pocket Album
Leicester
Leicestershire
Lincolnshire Living Memoires
Lincolnshire Pocket Album
Liverpool and Merseyside
London Pocket Album
Ludlow
Maidenhead
Maidstone
Malmesbury
Manchester Pocket Album
Marlborough
Matlock
Merseyside Living Memories
Nantwich and Crewe
New Forest
Newbury Living Memories
Newquay to St Ives
North Devon Living Memories
North London
North Wales
North Yorkshire
Northamptonshire
Northumberland
Northwich
Nottingham
Nottinghamshire Pocket Album
Oakham
Odiham Then and Now
Oxford Pocket Album
Oxfordshire
Padstow
Pembrokeshire
Penzance
Petersfield Then and Now
Plymouth
Poole and Sandbanks
Preston Pocket Album
Ramsgate Old and New
Reading Pocket Album
Redditch Living Memories
Redhill to Reigate
Richmond
Ringwood
Rochdale
Romford Pocket Album
Salisbury Pocket Album
Scotland
Scottish Castles
Sevenoaks and Tonbridge
Sheffield and South Yorkshire Pocket Album
Shropshire
Somerset
South Devon Coast
South Devon Living Memories
South East London
Southampton Pocket Album
Southend Pocket Album
Southport
Southwold to Aldeburgh
Stourbridge Living Memories
Stratford upon Avon
Stroud
Suffolk
Suffolk Pocket Album
Surrey Living Memories
Sussex
Sutton
Swanage and Purbeck
Swansea Pocket Album
Swindon Living Memories
Taunton
Teignmouth
Tenby and Saundersfoot
Tiverton
Torbay
Truro
Uppingham
Villages of Kent
Villages of Surrey
Villages of Sussex Pocket Album
Wakefield and the Five Towns Living Memories
Warrington
Warwick
Warwickshire Pocket Album
Wellingborough Living Memories
Wells
Welsh Castles
West Midlands Pocket Album
West Wiltshire Towns
West Yorkshire
Weston-super-Mare
Weymouth
Widnes and Runcorn
Wiltshire Churches
Wiltshire Living Memories
Wiltshire Pocket Album
Wimborne
Winchester Pocket Album
Windermere
Windsor
Wirral
Wokingham and Bracknell
Woodbridge
Worcester
Worcestershire
Worcestershire Living Memories
Wyre Forest
York Pocket Album
Yorkshire
Yorkshire Coastal Memories
Yorkshire Dales
Yorkshire Revisited

Frith Products & Services

Francis Frith would doubtless be pleased to know that the pioneering publishing venture he started in 1860 still continues today. Over a hundred and forty years later, The Francis Frith Collection continues in the same innovative tradition and is now one of the foremost publishers of vintage photographs in the world. Some of the current activities include:

Interior Decoration

Today Frith's photographs can be seen framed and as giant wall murals in thousands of pubs, restaurants, hotels, banks, retail stores and other public buildings throughout the country. In every case they enhance the unique local atmosphere of the places they depict and provide reminders of gentler days in an increasingly busy and frenetic world.

Product Promotions

Frith products are used by many major companies to promote the sales of their own products or to reinforce their own history and heritage. Frith promotions have been used by Hovis bread, Courage beers, Scots Porage Oats, Colman's mustard, Cadbury's foods, Mellow Birds coffee, Dunhill pipe tobacco, Guinness, and Bulmer's Cider.

Genealogy and Family History

As the interest in family history and roots grows world-wide, more and more people are turning to Frith's photographs of Great Britain for images of the towns, villages and streets where their ancestors lived; and, of course, photographs of the churches and chapels where their ancestors were christened, married and buried are an essential part of every genealogy tree and family album.

Frith Products

All Frith photographs are available Framed or just as Mounted Prints and Posters (size 23 x 16 inches). These may be ordered from the address below. From time to time other products - Address Books, Calendars, Table Mats, etc - are available.

The Internet

Already ninety thousand Frith photographs can be viewed and purchased on the internet through the Frith websites and a myriad of partner sites.

For more detailed information on Frith companies and products, look at this site:

www.francisfrith.com

See the complete list of Frith Books at:

www.francisfrith.com

This web site is regularly updated with the latest list of publications from The Francis Frith Collection. If you wish to buy books relating to another part of the country that your local bookshop does not stock, you may purchase on-line.

For further information, trade, or author enquiries please contact us at the address below:

The Francis Frith Collection, Frith's Barn, Teffont, Salisbury, Wiltshire, England SP3 5QP.

Tel: +44 (0)1722 716 376 Fax: +44 (0)1722 716 881 Email: sales@francisfrith.co.uk

See Frith books on the internet at www.francisfrith.com

FREE PRINT OF YOUR CHOICE

Mounted Print
Overall size 14 x 11 inches (355 x 280mm)

Choose any Frith photograph in this book.
Simply complete the Voucher opposite and return it with your remittance for £3.50 (to cover postage and handling) and we will print the photograph of your choice in SEPIA (size 11 x 8 inches) and supply it in a cream mount with a burgundy rule line (overall size 14 x 11 inches).
Please note: photographs with a reference number starting with a "Z" are not Frith photographs and cannot be supplied under this offer.
Offer valid for delivery to one UK address only.

***PLUS:* Order additional Mounted Prints at HALF PRICE - £7.49 each** (normally £14.99)
If you would like to order more Frith prints from this book, possibly as gifts for friends and family, you can buy them at half price (with no additional postage and handling costs).

***PLUS:* Have your Mounted Prints framed**
For an extra £14.95 per print you can have your mounted print(s) framed in an elegant polished wood and gilt moulding, overall size 16 x 13 inches (no additional postage and handling required).

IMPORTANT!

These special prices are only available if you use this form to order. You must use the ORIGINAL VOUCHER on this page (no copies permitted). We can only despatch to one UK address. This offer cannot be combined with any other offer.

Send completed Voucher form to:
The Francis Frith Collection, Frith's Barn, Teffont, Salisbury, Wiltshire SP3 5QP

CHOOSE A PHOTOGRAPH FROM THIS BOOK

for ***FREE*** *and Reduced Price Frith Prints*

Please do not photocopy this voucher. Only the original is valid, so please fill it in, cut it out and return it to us with your order.

Picture ref no	Page no	Qty	Mounted @ £7.49	Framed + £14.95	Total Cost £
		1	Free of charge*	£	£
			£7.49	£	£
			£7.49	£	£
			£7.49	£	£
			£7.49	£	£
			£7.49	£	£
			* Post & handling		£3.50
			Total Order Cost		£

Please allow 28 days for delivery.
Offer available to one UK address only

Title of this book ....
I enclose a cheque/postal order for £ ....
made payable to 'The Francis Frith Collection'

OR please debit my Mastercard / Visa / Maestro card, details below

Card Number

Issue No (Maestro only) Valid from (Maestro)

Expires Signature

Name Mr/Mrs/Ms ....
Address ....
....
....
.... Postcode ....
Daytime Tel No ....
Email ....

1-85937-281-3 Valid to 31/12/09

Free Print - see overleaf

Can you help us with information about any of the Frith photographs in this book?

We are gradually compiling an historical record for each of the photographs in the Frith archive. It is always fascinating to find out the names of the people shown in the pictures, as well as insights into the shops, buildings and other features depicted.

If you recognize anyone in the photographs in this book, or if you have information not already included in the author's caption, do let us know. We would love to hear from you, and will try to publish it in future books or articles.

Our production team

Frith books are produced by a small dedicated team at offices in the converted Grade II listed 18th-century barn at Teffont near Salisbury, illustrated above. Most have worked with The Francis Frith Collection for many years. All have in common one quality: they have a passion for The Francis Frith Collection. The team is constantly expanding, but currently includes:

Andrew Alsop, Paul Baron, Jason Buck, John Buck, Jenny Coles, Heather Crisp, David Davies, Natalie Davis, Louis du Mont, Isobel Hall, Chris Hardwick, Neil Harvey, Julian Hight, Peter Horne, James Kinnear, Karen Kinnear, Tina Leary, Stuart Login, Sue Molloy, Sarah Roberts, Kate Rotondetto, Eliza Sackett, Terence Sackett, Sandra Sampson, Adrian Sanders, Sandra Sanger, Julia Skinner, Lewis Taylor, Will Tunnicliffe, David Turner and Ricky Williams.